CALUMET CITY PUBLIC LIBRARY

3 1613 00490 5777

W9-DES-436

J
796.332
HOW

# CHICAGO BEARS

## BY BRIAN HOWELL

CALUMET CITY PUBLIC
LIBRARY

**The Child's World®**

Published by The Child's World®
1980 Lookout Drive • Mankato, MN 56003-1705
800-599-READ • www.childsworld.com

Acknowledgments
The Child's World®: Mary Berendes, Publishing Director
Red Line Editorial: Editorial direction
The Design Lab: Design
Amnet: Production

Design Element: Dean Bertoncelj/Shutterstock Images
Photographs ©: Paul Spinelli/AP Images, cover, 1; Charlie
Bennett/AP Images, 5; Football Hall of Fame/AP Images,
7; AP Images, 9; M. Spencer Green/AP Images, 11; Ed
Boettcher/Shutterstock Images, 13; Scott Boehm/AP
Images, 14–15; Phil Sandlin/AP Images, 17; David Goldman/
AP Images, 19; Nam Y. Huh/AP Images, 21; Vernon Biever/
AP Images, 23; John Bazemore/AP Images, 25; Scott
Grau/Icon Sportswire, 27; Reed Saxon/AP Images, 29

Copyright © 2016 by The Child's World®
All rights reserved. No part of this book may be
reproduced or utilized in any form or by any means
without written permission from the publisher.

ISBN 9781634070072
LCCN 2014959712

Printed in the United States of America
Mankato, MN
July, 2015
PA02265

## ABOUT THE AUTHOR

Brian Howell is a freelance writer based in Denver, Colorado. He has been a sports journalist for nearly 20 years and has written dozens of books about sports and two about American history. A native of Colorado, he lives with his wife and four children in his home state.

# TABLE OF CONTENTS

J
796.332
HOW

| | |
|---|---|
| GO, BEARS! | 4 |
| WHO ARE THE BEARS? | 6 |
| WHERE THEY CAME FROM | 8 |
| WHO THEY PLAY | 10 |
| WHERE THEY PLAY | 12 |
| THE FOOTBALL FIELD | 14 |
| BIG DAYS | 16 |
| TOUGH DAYS | 18 |
| MEET THE FANS | 20 |
| HEROES THEN | 22 |
| HEROES NOW | 24 |
| GEARING UP | 26 |
| SPORTS STATS | 28 |
| GLOSSARY | 30 |
| FIND OUT MORE | 31 |
| INDEX | 32 |

# GO, BEARS!

The Chicago Bears were one of the first professional football teams. They have won more games than any other team in the **league**. The Bears have won nine titles. Only the Green Bay Packers have won more. Chicago has had some of the best **defenses** ever. They also have a tradition that is tough to beat. Let's meet the Bears.

*The 1985 Chicago Bears defense is considered one of the best units of all time.*

# WHO ARE THE BEARS?

The Chicago Bears play in the National Football League (NFL). They are one of the 32 teams in the NFL. The NFL includes the American Football Conference (AFC) and the National Football Conference (NFC). The winner of the NFC plays the winner of the AFC in the **Super Bowl**. The Bears play in the North Division of the NFC. They have been to the Super Bowl twice. Chicago won it after the 1985 season. The Bears won seven NFL Championships before the Super Bowl began after the 1966 season. They also won an American Professional Football Association (APFA) title in 1921.

*Gale Sayers played just 68 NFL games but is still considered one of the best football players of all time.*

# WHERE THEY CAME FROM

The APFA began play in 1920. It became the NFL in 1922. The Decatur Staleys were one of the original APFA teams. They moved to Chicago in 1921. Then they became the Chicago Bears in 1922. George Halas was born in Chicago. He founded the team. Halas was a player and coach during the 1920s. He coached the Bears for 40 seasons. Halas retired in 1967. He remained the team's owner until his death in 1983.

*George Halas spent time as a player, coach, and owner of the Chicago Bears.*

# WHO THEY PLAY

The Chicago Bears play 16 games each season. With so few games, each one is important. Every year, the Bears play two games against each of the other three teams in their division. Those teams are the Detroit Lions, Green Bay Packers, and Minnesota Vikings. The Bears have been **rivals** with the Lions and Packers for more than 80 years. In fact, the Bears and Packers have the oldest rivalry in the NFL. They have played each other every year except one since 1921.

*The Bears and Packers have had many heated moments on the field since they started playing each other in 1921.*

# WHERE THEY PLAY

Soldier Field opened in 1924. The Bears made it their home in 1971. They played most of their games at Wrigley Field before that. Wrigley Field is home to the Chicago Cubs baseball team. Soldier Field is the oldest NFL stadium. It holds more than 61,000 fans. The stadium was remodeled in 2002.

*Soldier Field, the oldest NFL stadium, sits near Lake Michigan on the south side of Chicago.*

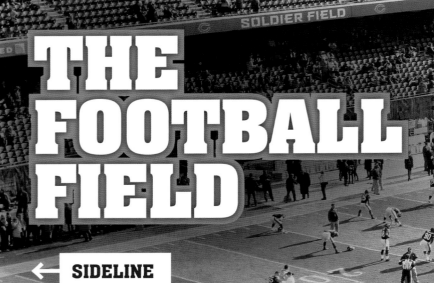

# THE FOOTBALL FIELD

← SIDELINE

HASH MARKS →

← GOAL LINE

← END ZONE

← END LINE

SOLDIER FIELD

MILLER LITE    CHASE    University of Phoenix    verizon

GOAL POST →

MIDFIELD

BENCH AREA

20-YARD LINE

15

# BIG DAYS

The Bears have had some great moments in their history. Here are three of the greatest:

**1940**—The Bears went 8-3 in the regular season. They met the Washington Redskins in the NFL Championship Game on December 8. It was no contest. Chicago won 73-0. That is still the biggest win in NFL history. It was Chicago's fourth title.

**1975**—Chicago drafted Walter Payton on January 28. He became one of the best running backs in NFL history. Payton made it to the **Pro Bowl** 9 times in his 13-year career. He was also the 1977 NFL **Most Valuable Player**.

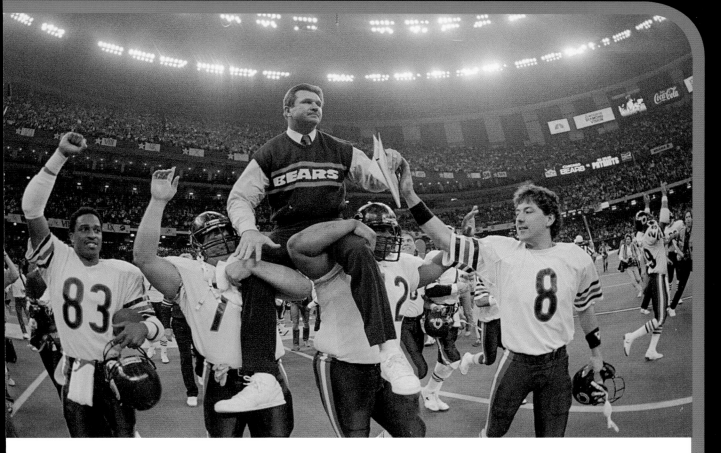

*Bears players carry coach Mike Ditka off the field after Chicago won its first Super Bowl, beating the New England Patriots 46–10 on January 26, 1986.*

**1985**—The 1985 Bears won the team's first Supr
on January 26, 1986. Chicago had mayb
defense ever. It allowed less than 1⁷
The Bears went 15-1 in the re
out the New England ™

3 1613 00490 5777

ᴀʀʏ

# TOUGH DAYS

ootball is a hard game. Even the best teams have rough games and seasons. Here are some of the toughest times in Bears history:

**1969**—Chicago had tough linebacker Dick Butkus. The Bears also had running back Gale Sayers. They are two of the best players in NFL history. But this was still Chicago's worst season ever. The Bears finished the season 1-13.

**2002**—The 2001 Bears had gone 13-3. Fans had high hopes for a great 2002. Chicago started 2-0. But then the Bears lost eight in a row. They finished the season 4-12.

*Marc Trestman (right), known for his offensive coaching ability, pulled quarterback Jay Cutler from the starting lineup during the Bears' disappointing 2014 season.*

**2014**—The 2013 Bears were the second-highest scoring team in the NFL. But the 2014 season was a disaster. Reporters heard players arguing with each other after games. The Bears finished 5–11. Coach Marc Trestman was fired after the season.

# MEET THE FANS

Chicago fans share their love for the Bears with their families. People in Chicago are known as tough and hard working. That is how the Bears have been viewed for years. The Bears have been in Chicago for more than 90 years. That has made a lot of fans stay loyal to the team. They like to call the team "Da Bears." That came from a famous sketch on the TV show *Saturday Night Live*.

*Fans pack the stands of Soldier Field to support the Bears during the frigid Chicago winters.*

# HEROES THEN

T he Bears have the most **Hall of Fame** players of any team through 2014. Dick Butkus was a Bears linebacker from 1965 to 1973. He is one of the toughest football players ever. Mike Singletary is another legendary Bears linebacker. Mike Ditka was a Hall of Fame tight end. But he is best known as a championship coach. He oversaw the team from 1982 to 1992. Chicago made the **playoffs** seven times in that span. That includes the Bears' Super Bowl win. Running backs Gale Sayers and Walter Payton are two of the best ever. Payton retired with 16,726 rushing yards. That was an NFL record at the time.

*Linebacker Dick Butkus made the Pro Bowl in eight of his nine NFL seasons.*

# HEROES NOW

**W**ide receiver Alshon Jeffery is a giant target. His size and big hands allow him to make great catches. He made the Pro Bowl in 2013. That was his second NFL season. He followed that with ten touchdown catches in 2014. Running back Matt Forte is another explosive offensive player. He runs and catches the ball well. Offensive lineman Kyle Long was good right away. He made the Pro Bowl as a rookie in 2013. He made it again in 2014.

*Wide receiver Alshon Jeffery makes a catch in a game against the Atlanta Falcons on October 12, 2014.*

# GEARING UP

NFL players wear team uniforms. They wear helmets and pads to keep them safe. Cleats help them make quick moves and run fast. Some players wear extra gear for protection.

## THE FOOTBALL

NFL footballs are made of leather. Under the leather is a lining that fills with air to give the ball its shape. The leather has bumps or "pebbles." These help players grip the ball. Laces help players control their throws. Footballs are also called "pigskins" because some of the first balls were made from pig bladders. Today they are made of leather from cows.

*Running back Matt Forte is one of the best pass-catching running backs in the NFL.*

26

HELMET

SHOULDER PADS

GLOVES

THIGH PADS

FOOTBALL

CLEATS

# SPORTS STATS

 **H**ere are some of the all-time career records for the Chicago Bears. All the stats are through the 2014 season.

## PASSING YARDS

Jay Cutler 18,725

Sid Luckman 14,686

## RECEPTIONS

Walter Payton 492

Matt Forte 443

## TOTAL TOUCHDOWNS

Walter Payton 125

Neal Anderson 71

## INTERCEPTIONS

Gary Fencik 38

Richie Petitbon 37

## SACKS

Richard Dent 124.5

Steve McMichael 92.5

## POINTS

Kevin Butler 1,116

Robbie Gould 1,080

*Running back Walter Payton ranks in the top five in career rushing yards and rushing touchdowns.*

## RUSHING YARDS

Walter Payton 16,726

Matt Forte 7,704

# GLOSSARY

**defenses** the units of a football team that try to keep the other team from scoring

**Hall of Fame** a museum in Canton, Ohio, that honors the best players

**league** an organization of sports teams that compete against each other

**Most Valuable Player** a yearly award given to the top player in the NFL

**playoffs** a series of games after the regular season that decides which two teams play in the Super Bowl

**Pro Bowl** the NFL's All-Star game, in which the best players in the league compete

**rivals** teams whose games bring out the greatest emotion between the players and the fans on both sides

**Super Bowl** the championship game of the NFL, played between the winners of the AFC and the NFC

# FIND OUT MORE

## IN THE LIBRARY

Editors of Sports Illustrated Kids. *Sports Illustrated Kids Football: Then to WOW!* New York: Sports Illustrated, 2014.

Frisch, Aaron. *Super Bowl Champions: Chicago Bears.* Mankato, MN: Creative Paperbacks, 2014.

McDill, Kent. *100 Things Bears Fans Should Know & Do Before They Die.* Chicago: Triumph Books, 2013.

## ON THE WEB

Visit our Web site for links about the Chicago Bears:
**childsworld.com/links**

*Note to Parents, Teachers, and Librarians: We routinely verify our Web links to make sure they are safe and active sites. So encourage your readers to check them out!*

# INDEX

American Football
  Conference (AFC), 6, 10
American Professional
  Football Association
  (APFA), 6, 8

Butkus, Dick, 18, 22

Chicago Cubs, 12

"Da Bears," 20
Decatur Staleys, 8
Detroit Lions, 10
Ditka, Mike, 22

Forte, Matt, 24

Green Bay Packers, 4, 10

Halas, George, 8

Jeffery, Alshon, 24

Long, Kyle, 24

Minnesota Vikings, 10

National Football Conference
  (NFC), 6, 10
National Football League
  (NFL), 6, 10, 12, 16, 18, 19,
  22, 26
New England Patriots, 17
NFC North, 6, 10
NFL Championship, 6, 16

Payton, Walter, 16, 22

*Saturday Night Live*, 20
Sayers, Gale, 18, 22
Singletary, Mike, 22
Soldier Field, 12
Super Bowl, 6, 17, 22

Trestman, Marc, 19

Washington Redskins, 16